# The Town
# That Moved

# The Town

story by Mary Jane Finsand

Carolrhoda Books ▪ Minneapolis, Minnesota

# That Moved

## pictures by Reg Sandland

*To Sister Martina Hughes
and the girls of the Class of 1921*

LIBRARY OF CONGRESS CATALOGING IN PUBLICATION DATA

Finsand, Mary Jane.
  The town that moved.

  (Carolrhoda on my own book)
  Summary: Describes how the houses and buildings
of a small town in northern Minnesota were moved
to another location when iron ore was discovered
in the ground beneath the town.
  1. Hibbing (Minn.) — History — Juvenile literature.
2. Moving of buildings, bridges, etc. — Juvenile
literature. [1. Hibbing (Minn.) 2. Minnesota —
History. 3. Moving of buildings, bridges, etc.]
I. Sandland, Reg, ill. II. Title. III. Series.
F614.H5F56     1983      977.6'77      82-9703
ISBN 0-87614-200-5

    2   3   4   5   6   7   8   9   10   90   89   88   87   86   85   84

# A Note from the Author

This is the story of a town named Hibbing, located in the middle of the great Mesabi Iron Ore Range in Minnesota. From its very beginning Hibbing depended upon the iron ore that surrounded it for its survival. So when iron ore was discovered right beneath the town, the solution was obvious: The town had to be moved. But how do you move a whole town? Even today it would be difficult, but in the early 1900s it seemed almost impossible. But the people of Hibbing were determined to save their town. This book tells the story of how they did it.

Some of this story comes from various newspaper accounts written at the time. Some of it comes from records kept by the Hibbing Historical Museum, the Hibbing Library, and the Minnesota Historical Museum. And a great deal of it comes from what people who lived in Hibbing when it moved have told me.

Once upon a time,
when the United States
was still a young nation,
much of the country was wilderness.
And so it was
in northern Minnesota.
What was there?
Forests and lakes.
Bears and deer and wolves.
Some men thought there might
even be gold and silver.
They were not sure,
but they were curious.
So they went to the wilderness
to seek their fortunes.

Some of these men
came to hunt the animals.
Then they sold the furs
to people in cities far away.

Others came to cut down trees
and sell the lumber.

Still other men came to look
for silver or gold.
They did not find much of either
in northern Minnesota.
They did not have
an easy life either!
There were no towns.
There were no roads.
The winters were long and cold.
It was no place to bring a family.
The men had to come
by themselves.

Then, in August of 1891,
a cyclone blew over the wilderness.

The winds were fast and strong.
They blew down many great trees.
Underneath,
on the roots of the trees
and in the holes they left behind,
men discovered iron ore!
There may not have been gold
in northern Minnesota,
but in the 1800s
iron ore was almost as exciting.
Iron ore is the rock
from which we get iron,
and in the 1800s
iron was badly needed
to build railroad trains and tracks.

It wasn't long before
news of the iron ore in Minnesota
had spread all around the country.
Men began to pour into Minnesota.
They came to start iron ore mines.
One of those men
was named Frank Hibbing.
Frank Hibbing knew
that if he started an iron ore mine
he would need many men
to work in it.
The men would want
to bring their families.
So Hibbing decided to
build a town.

First he bought land.

Then he hired men to build roads.

He hired other men
to build log cabins
for the families.

Soon people were coming
from all over the country
to work in Hibbing's mine
and live in his town.
People even came
from countries far away
like Ireland, Sweden, and Germany.
Many came to work in the mine,
but others came to open stores.
Soon there were schools
and churches and banks too.
On August 15, 1893,
the people voted to become
the town of Hibbing, Minnesota.

Hibbing became famous
for its rich iron ore.
The town grew and grew.
Everyone who lived there
was very proud of Hibbing.
They wanted to make it
a beautiful city.

They built fancy theaters
and lovely parks
and fine houses.
They started excellent schools
for their children,
and they took wonderful care
of their town.

Then one day
the mine owners made a discovery:
THE VERY BEST IRON ORE
WAS RIGHT BENEATH
THE TOWN OF HIBBING!
The people of Hibbing
would have to move.
If they didn't, the mines
would have to shut down.
The miners would be out of work.
Soon the other businesses
would have to close down too.

The people of Hibbing
were very upset.
They had worked so hard
to build their beautiful town.

How could they leave it?
How could they watch it
be torn down
to make way for new mines?

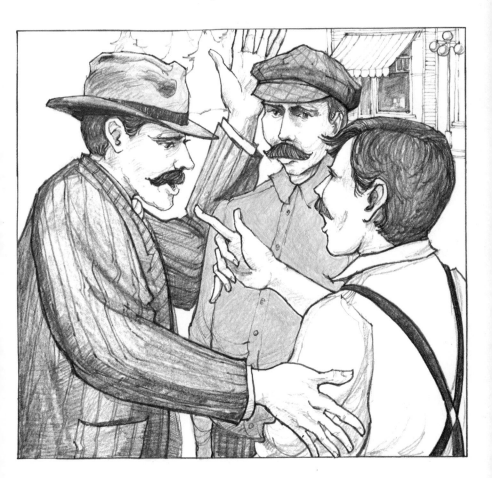

"Where will we go?" they asked.
"We will build you a new town,"
said the mine owners.
"But what about our fine homes
and our fancy theaters
and our beautiful hotels?"
the people asked.
The mine owners thought
and thought, and finally
they came up with a solution.
"We will move your homes!"
they said.
"We will move the whole town!"
It sounded like a wonderful idea.
But how on earth would they do it?

25

The mine owners and the people
sat down together to think and talk.
"We have horses and tractors,"
said one man.
"Maybe we could pull the buildings."
"But we can't pull big buildings
along the ground," said the mayor.
"They will break into pieces.
We need wheels or something."
"Wheels are a problem,"
said the mine owners.
"Most of our wheels
are just not large or strong enough
to move a building."

"Well," said someone else,
"we certainly have lots of trees.
We could cut them down,
then make them smooth
and roll our houses on them."
"That's it!" everyone cried.

So the mine owners and the people
began to get ready for moving day.
They separated all the buildings
from their basements.
Then they dug new basements
for all those buildings.

They chopped down trees.

Then they cut away the branches.

They made the logs smooth.

People all over the world
heard about Hibbing's plan to move.
"Impossible!" they said.
One big city newspaper wrote:
"HIBBING GONE CRAZY!"
No one believed
that the people of Hibbing
could move their whole town.

Finally moving day arrived.
The Hibbing Hotel would be
the first building moved.
The miners attached
large chains and ropes
to cranes from the mine.
The cranes would be powered
by steam engines.
Then the chains were wrapped
over and under the Hibbing Hotel.
Slowly the cranes lifted the hotel.
Then they swung it over
and lowered it gently
onto a log roller.

Next ropes and straps
were wrapped around the hotel,
then attached to horses up front.
"Giddap! Giddap!"
shouted the horse drivers.

The horses started forward.
Slowly the Hibbing Hotel
rolled down the street.

As soon as the back log
rolled out from under the building,
people grabbed it.

They strapped it to a horse
and pulled it up to the front.
Then they slid it underneath again.

After the Hibbing Hotel was moved,
they moved the Oliver Clubhouse.
The Oliver was so big,
it had to be cut in two parts
to move it.
Down the street
the buildings rolled
to their new locations.
Day in and day out
the people of Hibbing worked
to save their beautiful town.
At last all the business buildings
had been moved.
Next would come the houses.

"What should we do
with our furniture?"
the women asked.
"And our toys and clothes,"
said the children.
"Leave everything in the houses,"
they were told. "And you
can ride in your houses too."

43

The very next day
the first house
was lifted onto logs.
Down the street it came.

A log was placed up front.

Then a log rolled out back.

That log was placed up front,

and another log rolled out back.

And so it went until,
one after another,
186 houses had been moved.

The people of Hibbing
had done it!
They had moved their whole town!

# Afterword

Hibbing's move began in the year 1912, but the major push didn't come until 1921, and most of the buildings were moved in the 1920s. It wasn't until the fall of 1953 or the spring of 1954, though, that the very last building was finally moved.

The people of Hibbing moved their town because they loved it. It wasn't until many years later that they found they had made history. Today if you go to Hibbing you can see many of the buildings that were rolled on logs to where they now stand. And people are still proud to say, "We are from Hibbing, the town that moved!"